Pattern A

Enlarge pattern 200% for actual size.

Rendering

Ripples

The pieces for this picture frame are cut separately and then glued together in layers to form the frame. The waste material from Patter C should be saved and used as the panel at the back of the frame.

Enlarge patterns
200% for actual size.

Pattern A: Middle Layer

Pattern B: Top Layer

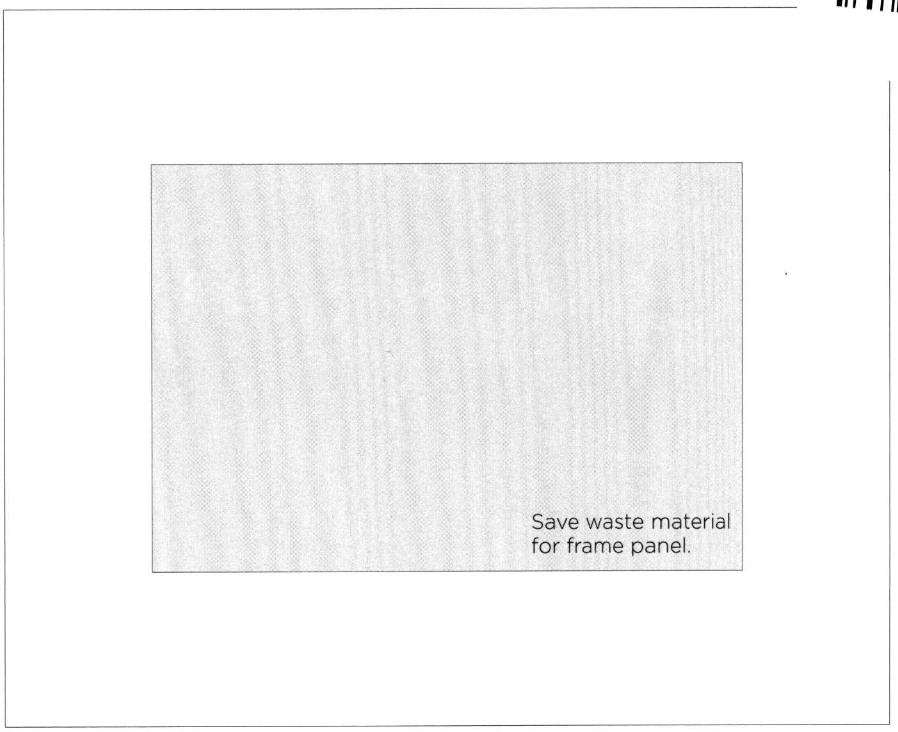

Pattern C: Bottom Layer

Enlarge patterns 200% for actual size.

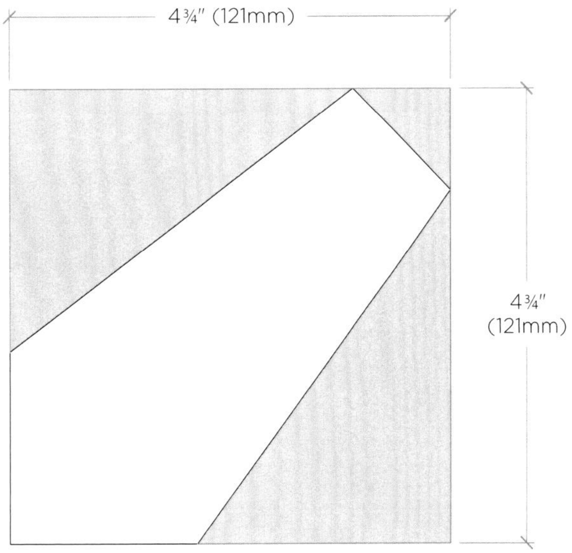

Pattern D: Frame Stand

Sun and Harvest

This project consists of four layers cut using Pattern A, an inlay piece of silver acrylic cut using Pattern A, and a final upper piece cut using Pattern B. To cut the project, stack four layers of wood together using double-sided tape. Attach Pattern A to the top of the stack. Cut the outline of the pattern and remove the bottom layer of wood from the stack so you have three layers remaining. Next, cut away the darkest areas of the pattern (see cutting chart for reference), and remove the bottom layer of wood from your stack so you have two layers remaining. Then, cut away the next darkest areas of the pattern (the areas within the rays and the inner circle connecting the rays). Separate the remaining two layers in your stack. Cut away any remaining shaded portions of the pattern from the top layer EXCEPT the center circle. The center circle is used to cut the acrylic inlay. Attach a sheet of silver acrylic to the underside of the top layer and cut away the center circle, creating the acrylic inlay. Use Pattern B to cut the final piece. Assemble the project by gluing and stacking the layers from bottom to top. Be sure to place the silver acrylic inlay in the top layer, and then glue Piece B in place over top of it.

Pattern B

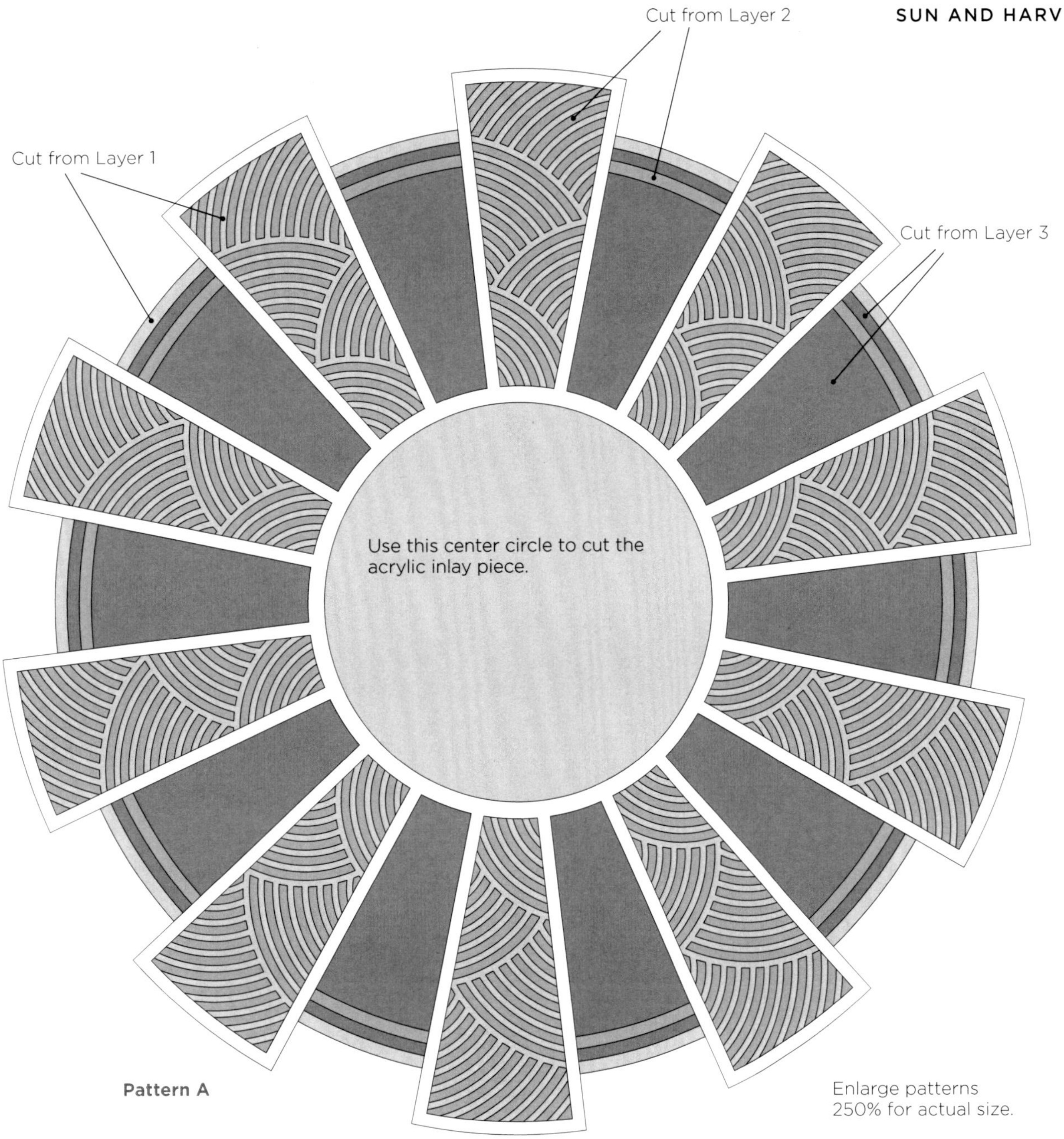

Cutting Chart

Layer 4 (bottom): Cut the outline of the pattern and remove Layer 4

Layer 3: Cut the darkest areas from the pattern (the sections between the rays)

Layer 2: Cut the next darkest areas from the pattern (the area within the rays and the inner circle connecting the rays)

Layer 1 (top): Cut away any remaining shaded areas of the pattern EXCEPT the center circle

Inlay: Attach a silver sheet of acrylic to the bottom of Layer 1 and cut away the center circle to form the inlay

Circular Void II

To cut this project, sandwich a thick layer of wood between two thinner layers of wood, using double-sided tape to hold the stack together. Attach the pattern. Cut the outline of the pattern. Then, cut away the darkest area of the pattern (the center circle). Remove the two thin, outer layers of wood from the stack and attach them to one another using double-sided tape. Cut away the remaining shaded areas of the pattern from the outer layers of wood. This project can also be cut with five layers as shown.

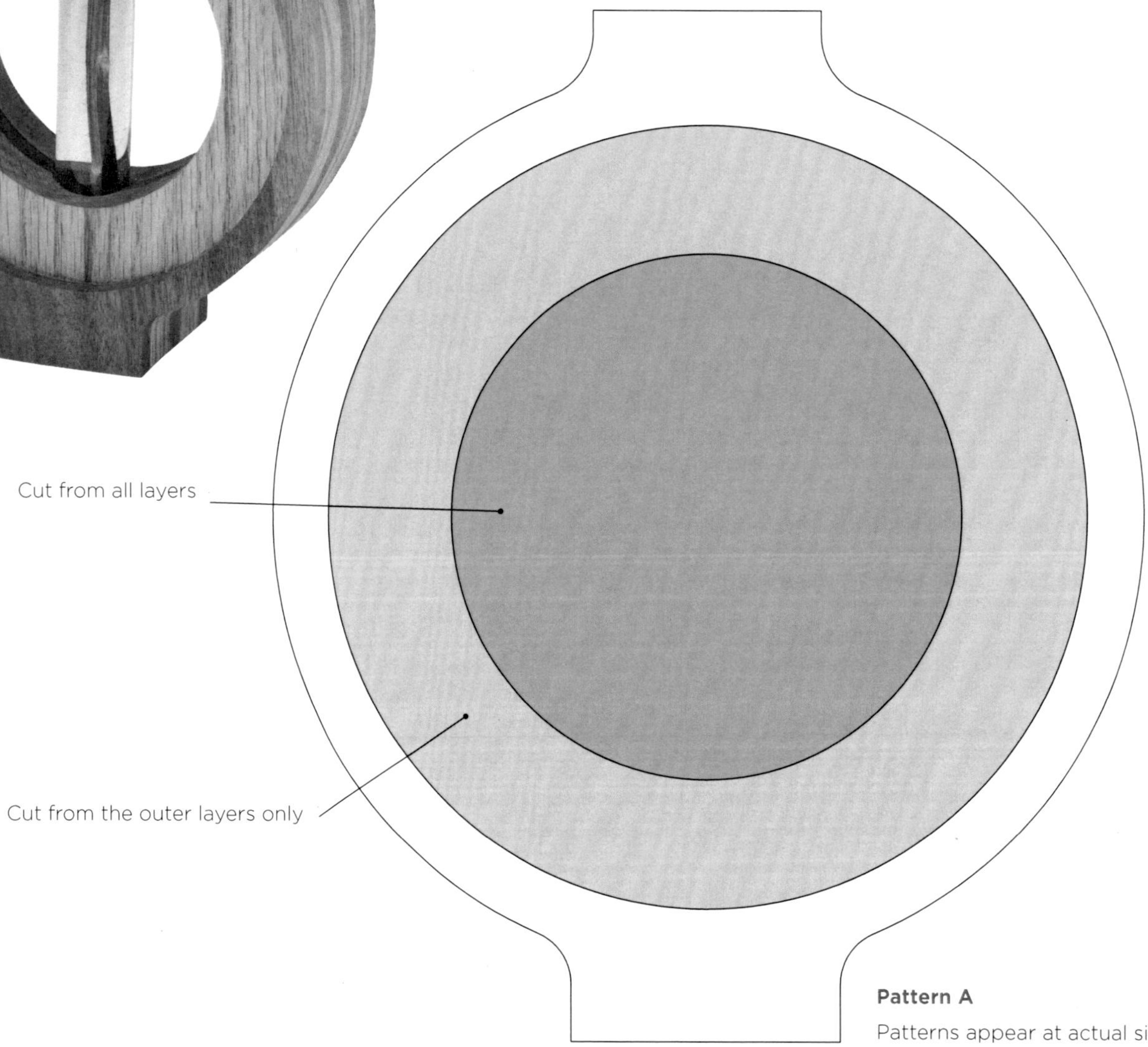

Pattern A

Patterns appear at actual size.

Geometrix II

This project consists of one piece cut with Pattern A, two pieces cut with Pattern B, and one piece cut with Pattern C. First, use Patterns A and C to cut their respective pieces. Then, attach Pattern B to one of the B pieces and sandwich the center spine of Piece A between the two B pieces. Secure the stack with double-sided tape. Cut the waste material from Pattern B, cutting through the two B pieces and the center spine of Piece A.

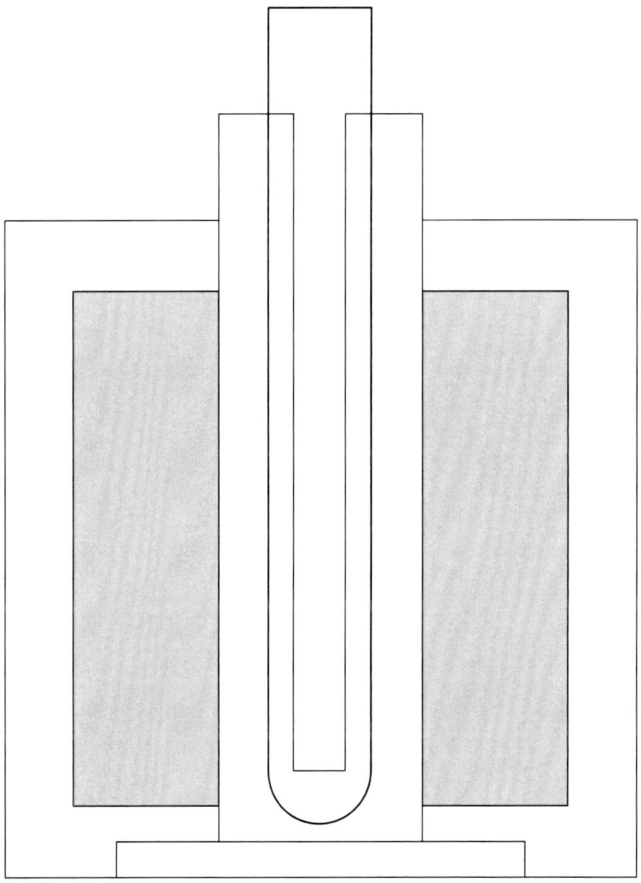

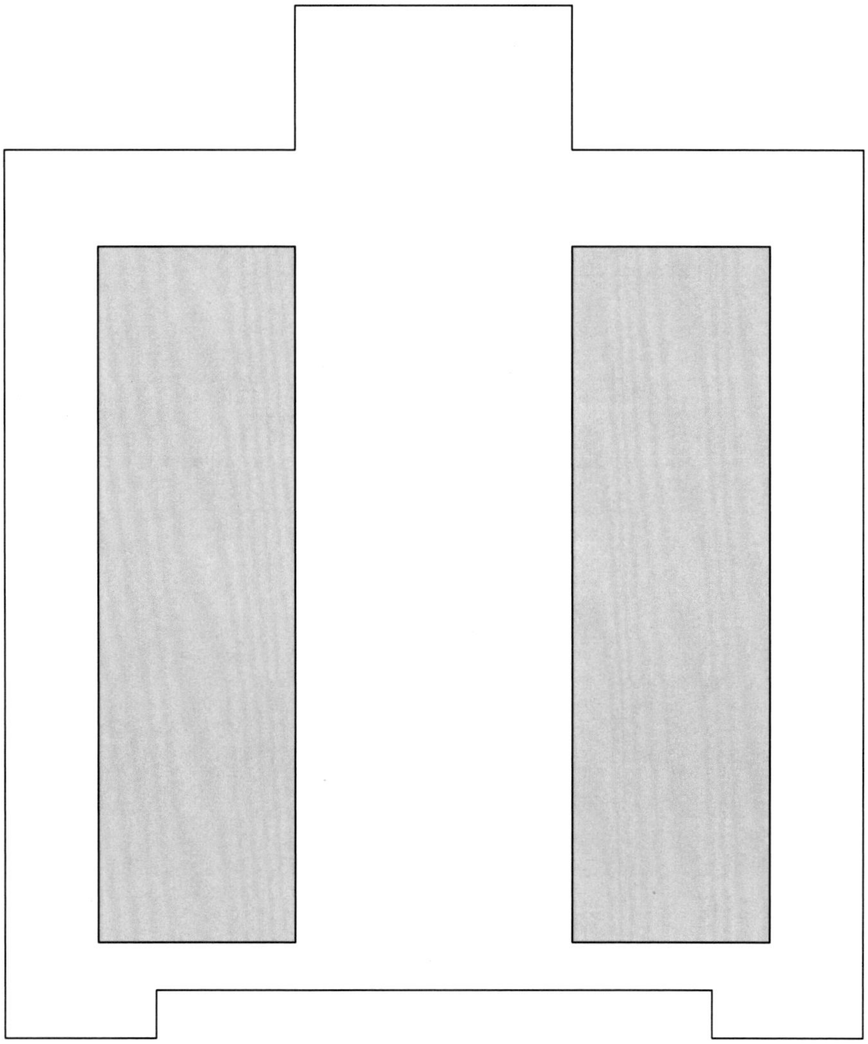

Pattern A

Patterns appear at actual size.

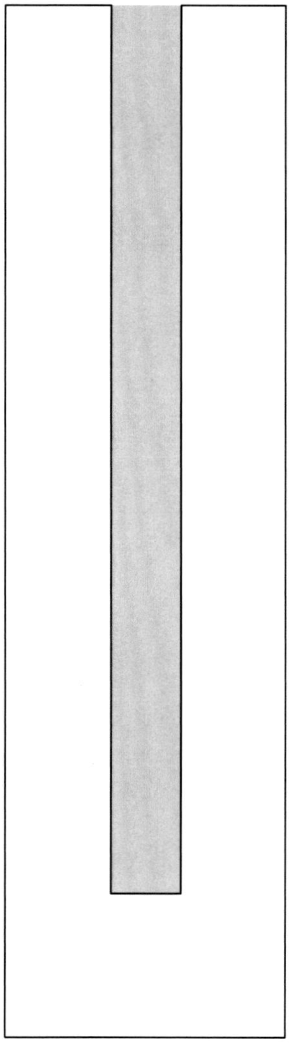

Pattern B

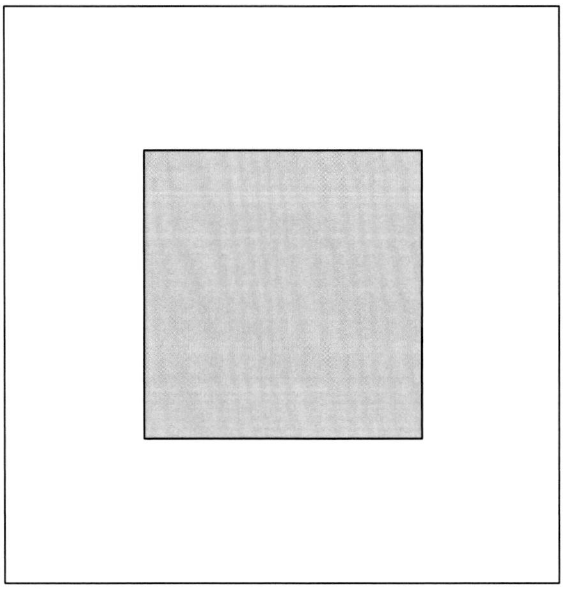

Pattern C

Ascending Spiral

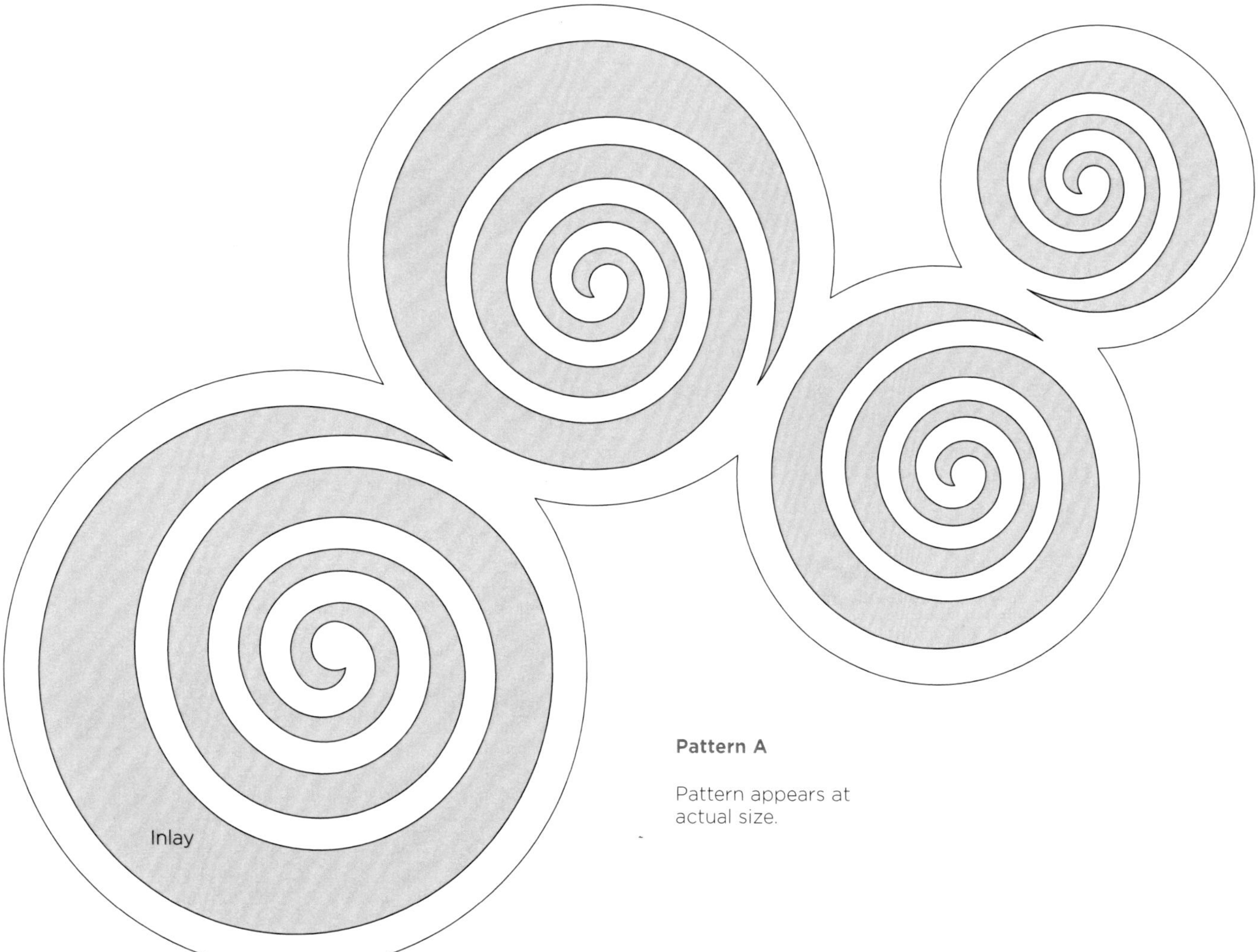

Pattern A

Pattern appears at actual size.

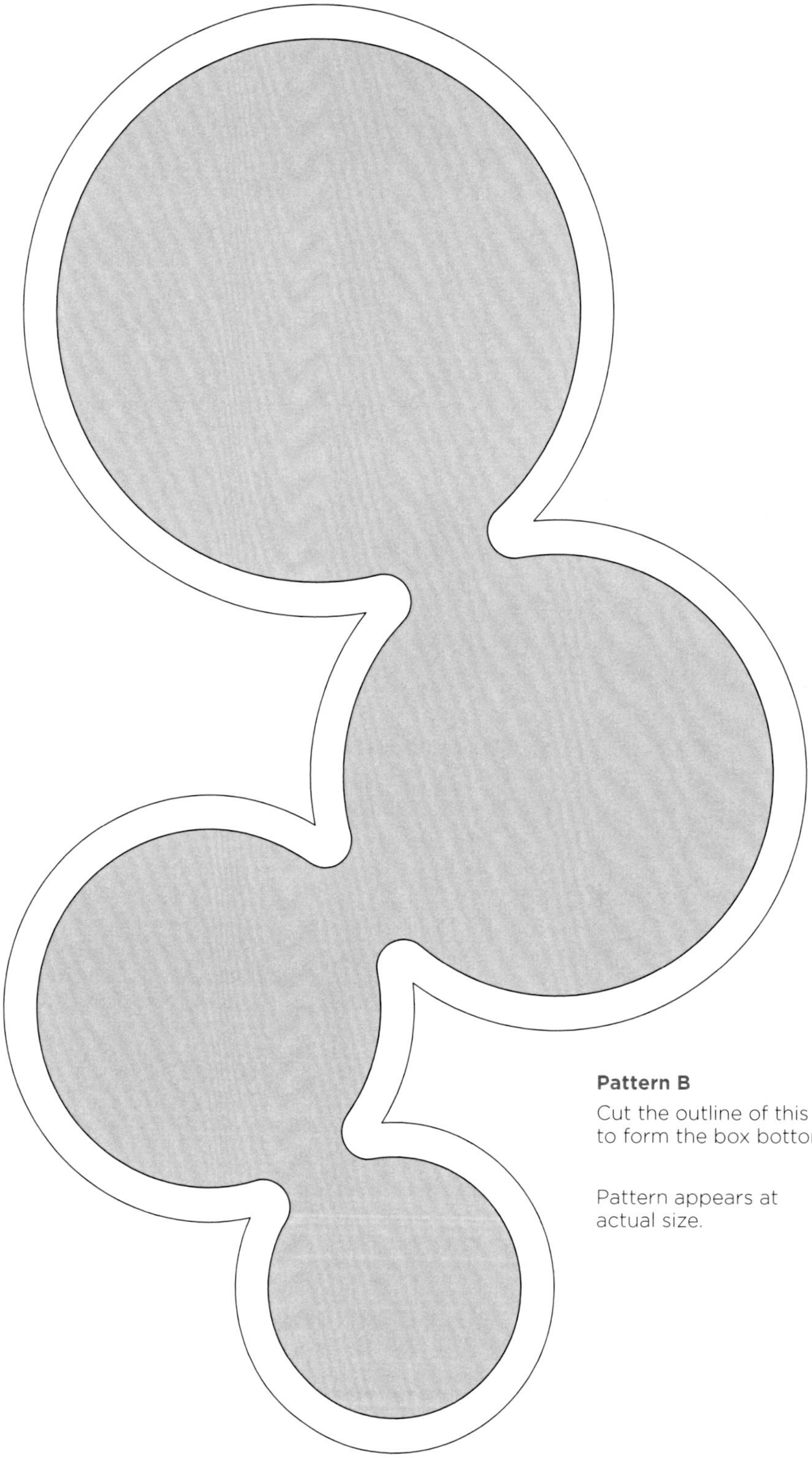

Pattern B

Cut the outline of this pattern to form the box bottom.

Pattern appears at actual size.

Spiraling Shape

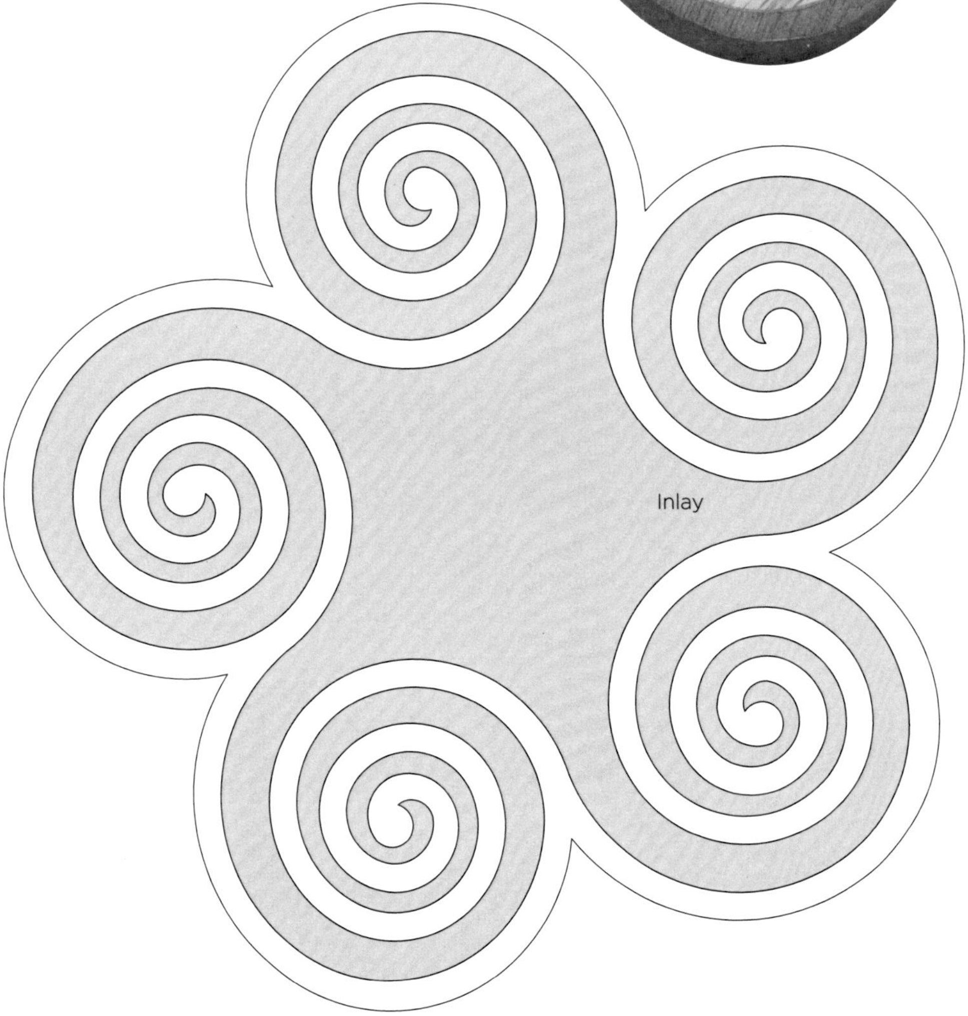

Pattern A

Pattern appears at actual size.

Pattern B

Cut the outline of this pattern to form the box bottom.

Pattern appears at actual size.

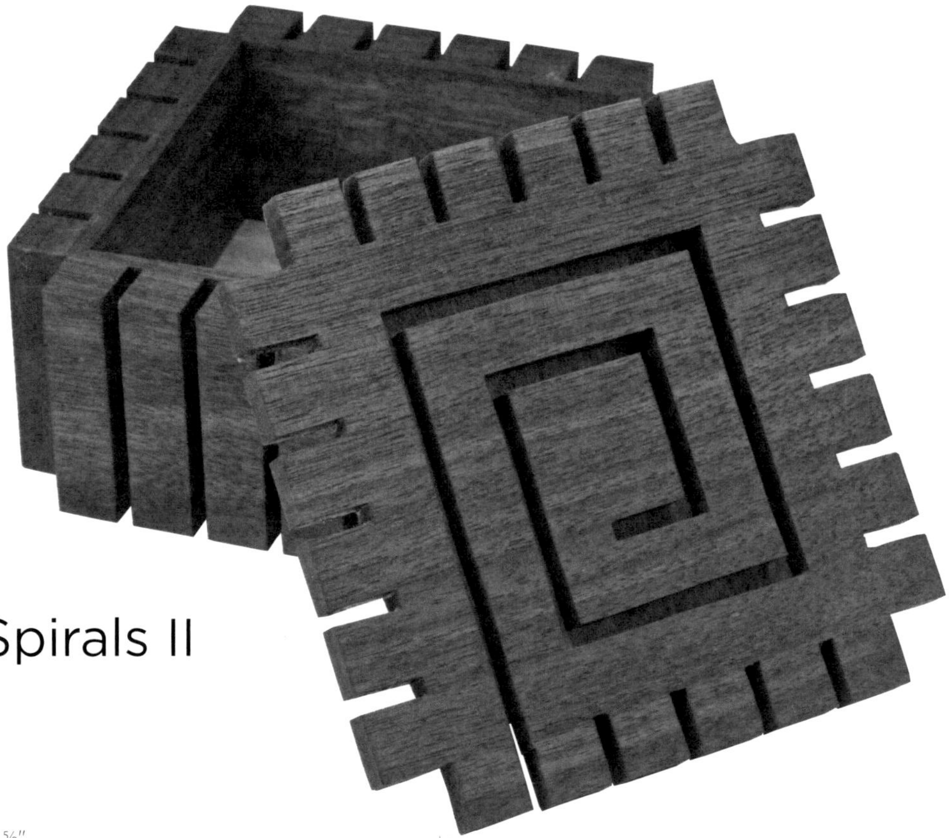

Rectilinear Spirals II

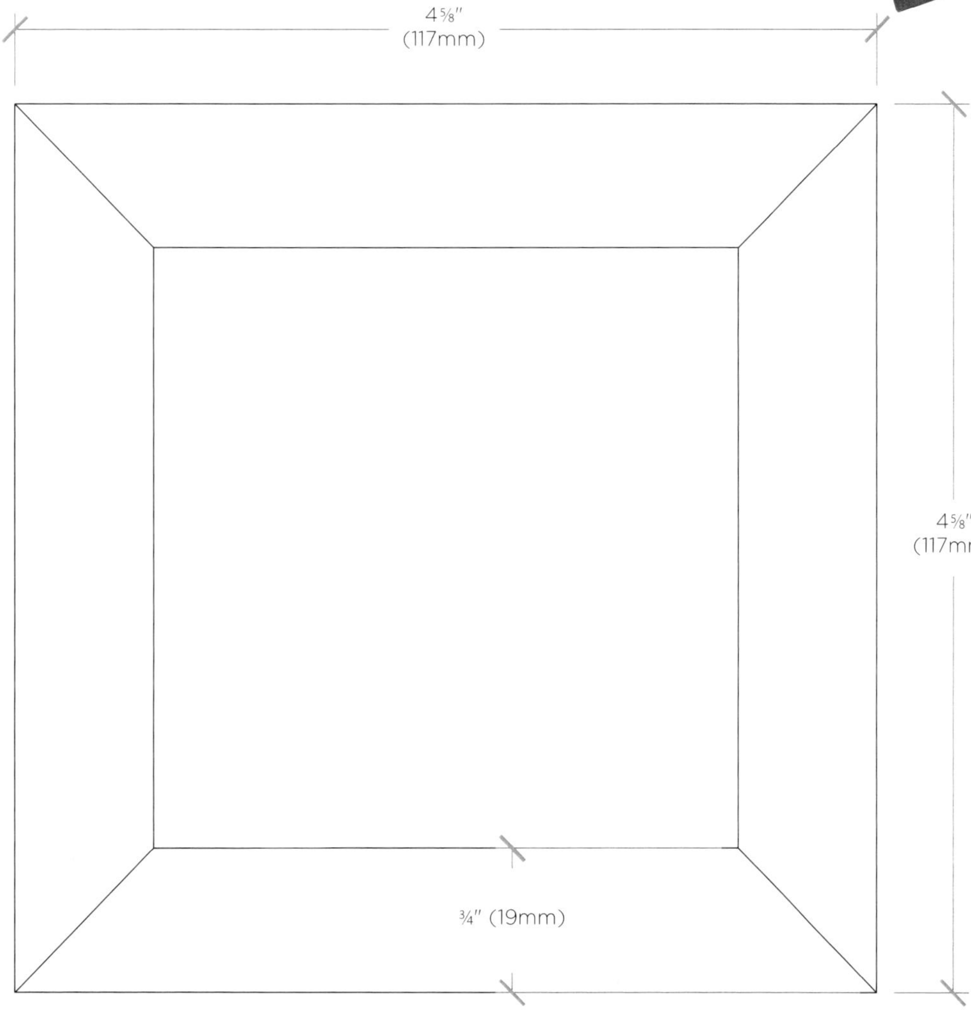

Inside View

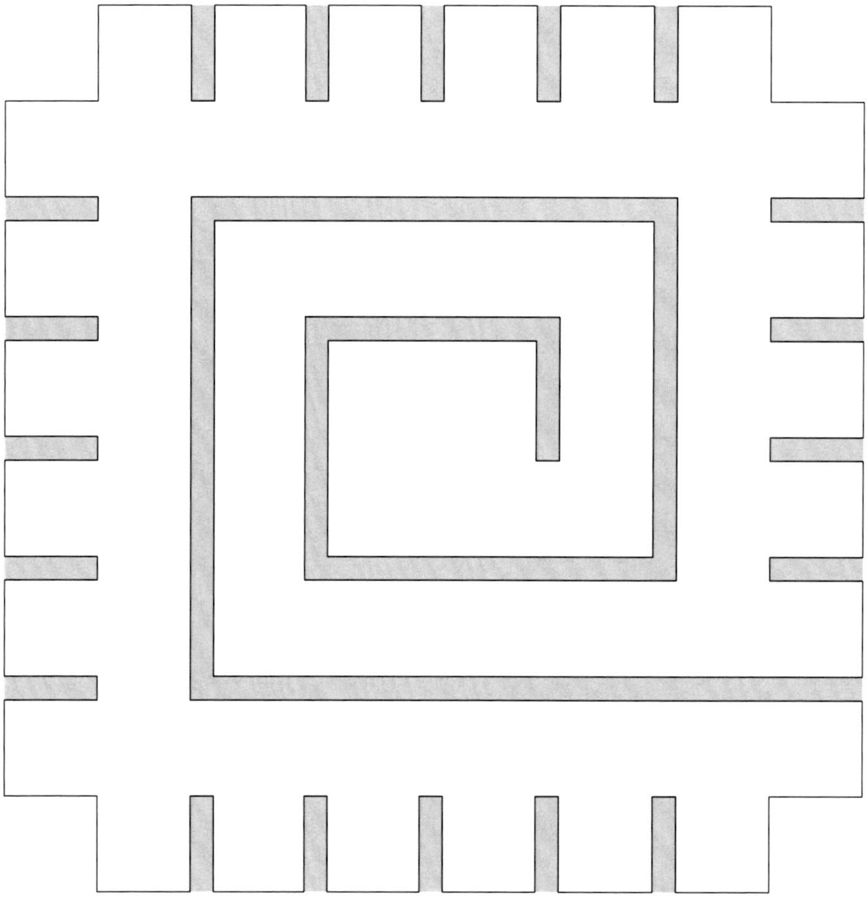

Pattern appears at actual size.

Pattern A

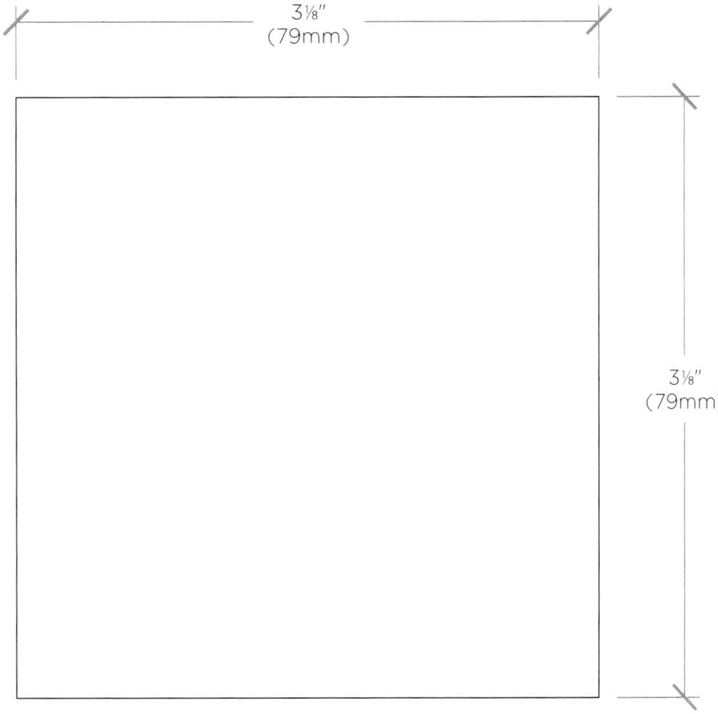

Pattern B: Lid Catch

Patterns appear
at actual size.

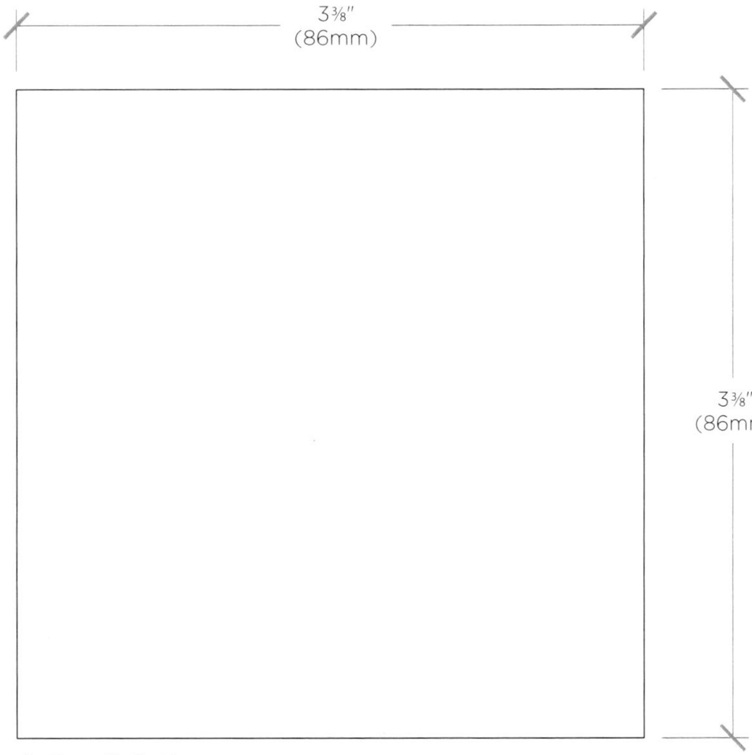

Pattern C: Bottom

4⅝"
(117mm)

Wright Inspired

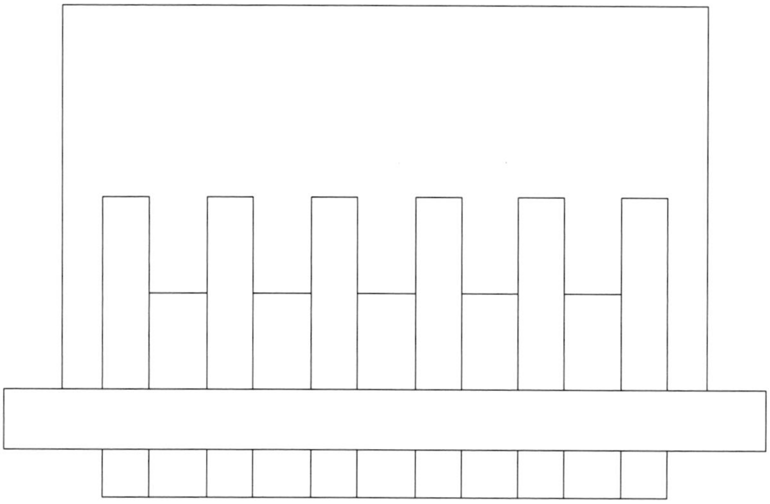

Rendering

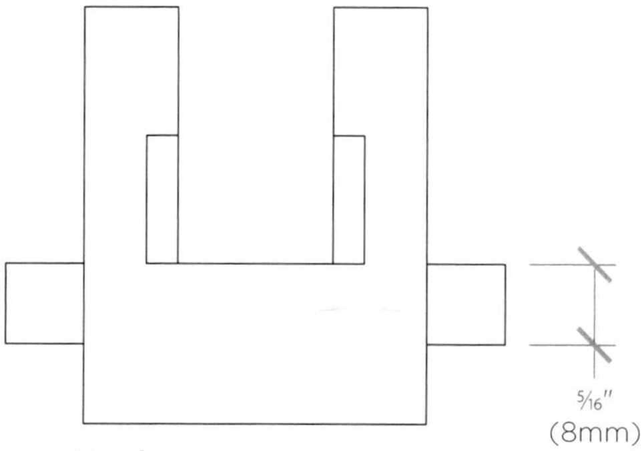

Section